# A Time To Be Born

Bible Lessons for the Growth of
Children's Faith

# A Time To Be Born

## Bible Lessons for the Growth of Children's Faith

Kay E. McNeil

**Ordering Information:**
Orders by U.S. trade bookstores and wholesalers. Quantity sales. Special discounts are available on quantity purchases by corporations, associations, and others. For details, contact the publisher at the following email address:

**Connect with Kay E. McNeil:**

**Email:**
ATimetoBeBornBook@gmail.com

Bible versions used for this book:

| | |
|---|---|
| Amplified Bible | AMP |
| King James Version | KJV |
| New International Version | NIV |
| New King James Version | NKJV |
| The Living Bible | TLB |
| Life Application Study Bible | LASB |
| American Standard Version | ASV |

# Author Bio

Kay E. McNeil has two passions: The first is teaching and training young children in the classroom. After teaching for forty-one years, Kay has now retired and is spending a lot of time enjoying her second passion: the writing of children's books. Kay lives a quiet peaceful life with her husband, Charles, in San Antonio, Texas.

Stay tuned for more books
in the *"A Time To …"* series
by Kay E. McNeil!

# Bible Verses to Remember

"Faith is something we hope for and something we want and expect, even though we cannot see it yet."
Hebrews 11:1 AMP

"Children obey your parents in the Lord: for this is right."
Ephesians 6:1 NKJV

"The righteous man walks in his integrity;
his children are blessed after him."
Proverbs 20:7 ASV

"And we know that all things work for good to those who love the Lord, and who are called according to his purpose."
Romans 8:28 NKJV

"Do not be afraid, stand still and see
the salvation of the Lord."
Exodus 14:13 NKJV

"The people fell on their faces, and said, the Lord He is God! The Lord He is God!"
1 Kings 18:39 KJV

"For God so loved the world, that He gave his only begotten son, that whosoever believeth in Him should not perish, but have everlasting life."
John 3: 16 KJV

# A Time to Be Born

Time is measured by using clocks and calendars. Clocks show seconds, minutes and hours. Calendars show days, weeks and months. Time always moves forward. We do not want to ever waste time, because we can never get it back.

# Dedication and Thanks

I dedicate this book to the memory of my daughter, Chasity Nicole McNeil. She listened to and obeyed her parents.

I also dedicate this book to all the youth who will read it.

Thank you to my husband, Charles, for helping me and praying for me as I worked on this wonderful project.

Thank you to Antoinette Griffith for writing the Foreword.

Thank you to Dr. Lisa Jennings for proofreading this book.

Thank you to Sharee Moore of Dynasty Publishers for self-publishing this book for us.

Thank you God for your Holy Spirit leading and guiding me throughout this journey. I could not have made it without your Love, Grace and Mercy. You are a constant presence.

# Foreword

Kay McNeil and I have been friends since the ninth grade. This deeply valued friendship expands over forty years. Like Kay, I also have a passionate love for children knowing Jesus Christ in a very intimate and personal way.

It has been Kay's dream and aspiration to one day write children's books that will motivate and encourage them to possess a yearning to know Jesus better. She wants children to read the Bible as if they were on a scavenger hunt and want to win the big prize! Kay has always emphasized that children need to know that reading the Bible is like watching a "good movie." There is action, drama, excitement, romance, and suspense!

In her various roles as a mother, educator of young children, homeschool teacher of her daughter Chasity, she has always exuded unconditional love, compassion, kindness and patience, while shaping and molding their young minds and hearts.

I know it is Kay's hope and prayer that as children read this book and get a glimpse of how the Lord worked in the lives of the noted Bible Characters (Abraham, Isaac, etc.), that they too will be Encouraged to read the Bible even more and develop a personal, vibrant relationship with the Father, Son, and Holy Ghost. Amen.

*Antoinette Griffin*

# Table of Contents

Author Bio ........................................................................ ix

Dedication and Thanks ................................................... xi

Foreword .........................................................................xiii

Introduction .................................................................. xvii

Chapter One - Abraham ................................................... 1

Chapter Two - Isaac ......................................................... 9

Chapter Three - Jacob .................................................... 17

Chapter Four - Joseph .................................................... 31

Chapter Five - Moses ..................................................... 53

Chapter Six - Elijah ........................................................ 71

Chapter Seven - Jesus .................................................... 81

# Introduction

Who said there is a time to be born? A man named Solomon (from the Bible) said it. In Ecclesiastes 3: 1-2, he says, "To everything there is a season, a time for every purpose under heaven. A Time to Be Born."

According to UN data, there are on average about 250 babies born every minute around the world. Even though that's a lot of babies, I am convinced that God has allowed every person to be born at the right time.

This book shows individuals from the Bible who God called for a special purpose. It also shows what took place in their lives, as they grew and matured, and as they experienced defeat and victory. Some lost their faith for a time. And other times, their faith in God was overwhelmingly strong.

Abraham - Father of Faith and The Father of Many Nations.

Isaac - Son of Promise and The Father of Many Nations.

Jacob - The Father of Many Nations whose sons became the Twelve Tribes of Israel.

Joseph – Favorite son of Jacob. He became the second in command of Egypt. He went from Riches-Rags-Riches.

Moses – The Deliverer of God's People.

Elijah – Prophet of God. Born to Reveal God's Word.

Jesus - The Son of God. He had an Amazing and Celebrated Birth.

<u>Words to know</u> - Will come before each chapter
<u>A Special Feature</u> – Will come after each chapter
<u>Scripture references</u> – Will come after each chapter
<u>Chapter review</u> - Will come after each chapter

As you read this book, may you develop a healthy self-esteem. It is unnecessary to compare yourself to others. For God created you and allowed you to be born for a <u>special purpose</u>. You only need to find it, believe it, and live it.

# 1

# Abraham

## Words to Know

| | |
|---|---|
| **Ai:** | A place in Canaan, now Israel. |
| **Almighty:** | Strong and powerful. |
| **Altar:** | A place set apart to pray and honor God. |
| **Bethel:** | A place in Canaan, now Israel. |
| **Birth:** | The emergence of a new individual from the body of its mother. |
| **Bless:** | Good things for a person. |
| **Burnt Offering:** | A sacrifice (usually bulls, sheep and goats, turtle doves and pigeons) offered to God and burned typically on or at an altar. |
| **Canaan:** | Located in the Middle East. The promised land for Abraham's descendants and God's chosen people. Also, a part of Southwest Asia. |
| **Covenant:** | A promise between two or more. |

**Curse:** Bad things for a person.

**Descendants:** Persons born from their parents, grandparents, etc.

**Egypt:** A place south of Israel.

**Faith:** To believe strongly in someone or something.

**Flint:** An item used to make tools and for starting fires.

**God:** The Creator of heaven and earth.

**Greatly:** Very much.

**Hebrew:** A race of people. God's chosen people.

**Heir:** A person who receives possessions from a person or persons who have died.

**Inheritance:** Property or possessions you get from a person who have died or will die soon.

**Multiply:** An increase or more of what you already have.

**Nation:** A group of people living in the same society or sharing the same language, race etc.

**Negev:** A place in Canaan, now called Israel.

**Patriarch:** The male head of a family.

**Possessions:** All the things you own.

**Pregnant:** When a female has a baby in her belly.

**Righteous:** A good person according to God.

**Sacrifice:** Giving something up that you have that's special to you.

**Servants:** People who work for others, sometimes without pay.

# 1

## Abraham
### Father of Faith and Father of Many Nations

A bram was born and grew up in the city of UR. Sometime after marriage, he and his wife Sarai moved to a place called Haran. This is where Abram's family lived. One day God came to Abram and said, "Leave your country, your people, and your father's family. I want you to go to a land that I will show you." God also said, "I will make you a great nation! I will bless all those who bless you. And I will curse anyone who curses you! All families on earth, shall be blessed through you!"

Abram was truly a man of faith. He obeyed God and left his homeland. He took his wife Sarai, his nephew Lot, and all their possessions and servants, and left Haran. Abram was seventy-five years old at the time.

After leading Abram to the land of Canaan, God again appeared to him. He said, "I will give this land to your descendants." Abram built an altar there to show respect and honor to God.

Abram and Lot were both very wealthy men. They had plenty of animals such as flocks of sheep and herds of cattle. Abram even had camels, donkeys, silver and gold. They both had servants and tents. But they did not have enough land space for all their animals, causing their servants to fight with each other. One day Abram suggested he and Lot separate. Abram gave Lot the first choice of land. So Lot picked the fertile plain of Jordan. He traveled east and lived near the wicked city of Sodom. Abram stayed in the land of Canaan.

When Abram was ninety-nine years old, God came to him again. He said, "I am God Almighty. Be obedient to me always and I will make a covenant between you and me. I will greatly multiply your descendants. I am changing your name from Abram to Abraham because you will be a father of many nations. Kings will come from you."

God also changed Abraham's wife Sarai's name to Sarah, meaning princess. God told Abraham He would bless Sarah and give him a son from her. She would be a mother of many nations.

Abraham and Sarah both laughed at the thought of having a baby in their old age. They forgot that nothing is too hard for God. God also told Abraham to name their son Isaac, which means laughter in Hebrew. God said to Abraham, "Next year, I will give you and Sarah a son."

God did exactly what he promised: Sarah gave birth to a son and Abraham named him Isaac. Abraham was one-hundred years old and his wife Sarah was ninety years old.

Abraham and Sarah probably looked at their baby boy with joy as they each took a turn holding him for the first time. This baby was loved and very special to them because they waited a long time for God to give him to them. Isaac soon grew into a healthy and obedient young lad.

One day, God decided to test Abraham's faith. He told him to sacrifice his son Isaac. No doubt Abraham was very sad and thought surely God would not want Isaac, his promised son, to be hurt. But Abraham trusted and obeyed God anyway. Abraham took Isaac to Mount Moriah, the place where God told him to make the sacrifice. Abraham built an altar there and placed wood on top of it. He then tied Isaac's hands together and laid him on top of the wood. Abraham took out a knife and was about to sacrifice his son! But an angel of the Lord stopped him saying, "Abraham! Abraham! Do not hurt your son! Now I know you fear God, because you were willing to give up the son whom you love so much!"

I imagine Abraham was so glad that God spared his son's life! Abraham saw a ram with its horns stuck in a bush. So, Abraham took the ram and offered it to God as a burnt offering instead of his son. Abraham named that place "The Lord Will Provide."

The Bible does not discuss the events surrounding Abraham's birth. But the time of his call was perfect, for two reasons. First, God used Abraham's strong faith to show the world how important faith is for everyday living. In Hebrews 11:1, we read that faith is something we hope for and something we want and expect even though we cannot see it yet. Second, God called Abraham to be the Patriarch for God's chosen people. God once told Abraham that his descendants would be like the stars in the sky and the sand on the beach.

Abraham was known as the Father of Faith, because he always trusted and obeyed God. And because of this, God made him a Father of Many Nations.

# Special Feature

**A few of Abraham's Journeys**

These places and others are found throughout Genesis 12:1 and 25:1-11.

Ur of the Chaldeans
Haran
Shechem
Between Bethel and Ai
Negev
Egypt
Hebron

# Scripture References

Genesis 12: 1-7
Genesis 13: 8-13
Genesis 17: 1, 2, 5, 6, 15, 16, 17
Genesis 18:12
Genesis 21: 1, 2, 3, 5
Genesis 22: 1-14

# Chapter Review

1. Obedience is not always easy. Do you think it was hard or easy for Abraham to leave his family and country?

2. Why did Abraham's servants fight with Lot's servants?

3. What did Abraham have to do for God to make a covenant between the two of them?

4. What is the meaning of Sarah's name?

5. What did Sarah and Abraham laugh about?

6. Who told Abraham not to hurt his son?

7. True or false: Abraham offered a bull to God as a burnt offering to God.

# 2

# Isaac

## Words to Know

**Angel of the Lord:**  A spiritual being that God sends down to earth to deliver a message to someone.

**Barren:**  A woman unable to have a baby.

**Bride:**  A woman who will get married.

**Complaining:**  Expressing displeasure or disappointment in something.

**Famine:**  No plant can grow for food because of dry land; no rain or water.

**Idol:**  A thing that is worshipped other than God.

**Plunge:**  To suddenly jump, dive, penetrate into something.

**Recited:**  To say something over and over again.

**Socialize:**  Talking and communicating with other people.

9

**Thrilled:** Very, very happy and excited.

**Troubling:** Causing a person to feel stress, worried or confused.

**Weaned:** No longer drinking breast milk from a mother.

**Well:** A hole dug in the ground to hold a large amount of water.

**Worship:** To show reverence, adoration and honor to something or someone.

# 2

## Isaac
## The Son of Promise and Father of Many Nations

At last Abraham and Sarah had their promised son, Isaac. Isaac was the first son born to his mother Sarah, but the second son born to his father Abraham. Isaac's fourteen-year-old half-brother was named Ishmael.

As time passed, Isaac was weaned, and his father gave him a party. But while at the party, Isaac's mother Sarah saw Ishmael and his mother teasing little Isaac. Isaac's mother did not like that. So, Sarah told her husband Abraham to send the two of them away. Sarah did not want Ishmael to be Abraham's heir with her son Isaac. Abraham was sad and did not want to do this, but God comforted him. "He said, listen to Sarah your wife and do what she says. For my promise of many descendants will come through your son Isaac. But I will also make a nation of Ishmael's descendants."

Isaac was an obedient son, even in that moment when his father was about to offer him up to God. God told Abraham to sacrifice Isaac and use him as a burnt offering to God. Well, instead of protesting, it seemed as if Isaac obeyed his father.

I think about the Bible verse found in Ephesians 6:1. It says, "children obey your parents in the Lord: for this is right."

The Bible does not record too much of what Isaac said or did. It mainly tells us that Isaac was a very obedient son.

As Isaac lay on top of the wood, God sent an Angel just in time to stop Abraham from sacrificing his son! God showed Abraham a ram whose horns were trapped in a bush. Abraham went and got the ram and sacrificed it instead of his son Isaac.

When Isaac was thirty-seven years old, his mother Sarah died. This was a very sad time for Isaac. So Abraham sent his servant Eliezer to find a wife for Isaac. Abraham did not want Isaac to marry a Canaanite woman because so many of them worshiped idols. Abraham said to his servant, "Go back to my country Haran and pick a wife from among my family."

Eliezer left Canaan with ten of Abraham's camels loaded with lots of gifts. The gifts were for the bride and her family.

Abraham's servant Eliezer traveled for many days and finally arrived in Haran. As he stood by a well, Eliezer prayed about what he had to do. While still praying, a beautiful young woman came to the well. When Eliezer asked the woman for a drink, she gave it to him. But she also offered to get water for his camels. Eliezer was so pleased, because she did exactly what he prayed. Eliezer knew this was the woman for Isaac. So Eliezer gave the young woman a gold ring and two bracelets.

Then he asked, "Whose daughter are you? And does your father have enough room for me and the rest of the servants to stay?" The young woman said, "Bethuel is my father and my grandparents are Nahor and Milcah. I am Rebekah! We have straw and food for your camel and a room for you to stay in!" Eliezer worshipped and thanked God for bringing him to his master's family! It was the home of Abraham's very own brother, Bethuel!

Rebekah ran home to tell her family about what happened at the well! She had a big brother named Laban, who saw the ring and bracelets on her. He also listened to her story. Laban ran out to the well where Eliezer was standing and invited him to their home. Laban unloaded the camels, gave them straw to lie on and food to eat. Laban also got water ready to wash the servant's feet and all the men that were with him. Laban offered Eliezer food, but the servant did not want to eat until he told them why he was there.

Eliezer spoke saying, "I am Abraham's servant. My master is very rich with silver, gold, flocks of sheep and goats, herds of cattle, camels and donkeys. His wife has died and now he wants a wife for his son, Isaac. My master made me promise to get Isaac a wife from his father's house. So here I am. Let me know what you will do."

Rebekah's father Bethuel and her brother Laban agreed to let Rebekah go. Both men agreed that what Eliezer said was from God. They said, "Take her and give her to your master's son."

Eliezer was so thrilled that he worshipped God. Then he gave Rebekah and her family silver and gold jewelry and clothes. Everyone in the house sat down to eat and socialize with each other all night.

The next morning Rebekah, her nurse, Eliezer, and his men left Haran. They were headed back to Canaan to give Isaac his bride. Rebekah's family recited a blessing over her life before they left.

After many days of traveling, Rebekah, Eliezer, and the whole group arrived in Canaan. About this same time, Isaac went out to the fields and saw camels coming his way. Rebekah and her traveling group were headed towards Isaac. Rebekah asked Eliezer, "Who is that man coming our way?" "It is Isaac, my master's son," said Eliezer. When Isaac reached the group, Eliezer introduced Isaac to Rebekah, and then told him all about the trip. Isaac was forty years old when he married Rebekah. He then felt much better about his mother's death.

Isaac knew he was the Son of Promise, and that many descendants would come from him. Once God appeared to him saying, "Do not go down to Egypt. Stay in this land of Canaan for a while. I will be with you and bless you. I will make your descendants as many as the stars in the sky. And I will give them all of this land. All the nations on earth will be blessed because your father Abraham obeyed me."

Some people may think that Isaac's birth came too late in his parent's life. But he was born right on time to fulfill God's purpose for him. Isaac was the heir of all that his father Abraham owned: Including God's promise that he would be a Father of Many Nations.

# Special Feature

**Isaac was a unique man.**
He was born of old, loving parents.
He was obedient to his parents.
He grew up with a strong father, whose faith was in God Almighty. Abraham was a good example before his son Isaac.
He showed quiet courage when his father attempted to offer him as a sacrifice at God's request.
He trusted another man to choose a wife for him.
He inherited much wealth from his parents.
He lived to the old age of 180 years old.

# Scripture References

Genesis 21: 1-13
Genesis 22: 1-14
Genesis 24: 1-10
Genesis 24: 23-27
Genesis 24: 28-38
Genesis 24: 50-54
Genesis 24: 59-67
Genesis 25: 20
Genesis 26: 2-5

# Chapter Review

1. Why did Sarah have Isaac's older brother sent away?

2. How old was Isaac when his mother died?

3. Why did Eliezer give Rebekah a gold ring and two bracelets?

4. Who was Rebekah's father and who were her grand-parents?

5. Eliezer did not want to eat until when?

6. What did Rebekah's family do before she left with Eliezer?

7. God told Isaac that he would make his descendants as many as what?

# 3

# Jacob

## Words to Know

| | |
|---|---|
| **Aged:** | An individual who has gotten older. |
| **A Tenth:** | 10% of something. |
| **Barren:** | A woman unable to have a baby. |
| **Birthright:** | A special blessing from parents, usually from the father. An heir to the father's possessions when he dies. It is usually given to the first-born son. |
| **Bowed:** | To bend the head, body, or knee before a person to show respect. |
| **Con artist:** | A person who cheats or tricks someone. They convince others to believe a lie. |
| **Deceive:** | To tell a lie. |
| **Famine:** | Dry ground, because of no rain. Crops used for food will not grow. |
| **Favor:** | Gaining approval or acceptance. |
| **Father-in-law:** | The father of someone's husband or wife. |

**Fertile:** Rich land; plenty of rain and sun to grow crops; a woman that's able to have babies.

**Hinder:** To stop or block someone or something from getting by or through.

**Idols:** Persons or things that are loved more than God.

**Nations:** Groups of people living together in a particular place, country or territory.

**Nursing:** When a baby drinks milk from his or her mother.

**Pillar:** A big stone or rock to symbolize strength; a place where God speaks.

**Possess:** To have or own something.

**Pregnant:** When a woman has a baby inside of her body.

**Righteous:** A good person.

**Serve:** To do particular things for others. For example, to bring someone a drink of water; also to work for someone for free.

**Socialize:** Spending time talking and communicating with others.

**Struggle:** A strong effort to get free from restraint.

**Suffer:** A bad or unpleasant experience.

**Trials:** A test; a series of negative or sorrowful events.

**Trickster:** A person who cheats and lies to others.

**Uncontrollable:** An individual who cannot stop themselves or cannot be stopped by others.

**Urging:** A person trying to convince others to do something.

# 3

## Jacob

### Father of Many Nations Whose Sons Became the Twelve Tribes of Israel

After nineteen years of marriage, Isaac and Rebekah's twin sons were born. The first to come into the world had red hair all over his body. He was named Esau. When the second baby was born, he was holding onto his brother's heels. He was named Jacob. Their father Isaac was sixty years old at the time.

Esau and Jacob grew up with different personalities. Esau spent his time outdoors hunting in the fields, while Jacob spent a lot of his time inside and around the tent. Each son was favored by a different parent. Isaac was closest to Esau and Rebekah was closest to Jacob.

One day, Jacob was outside the tent cooking stew when his brother Esau came home from the fields. Esau was very tired and hungry and asked Jacob for some stew. "Sure, I'll give you some, but first sell me your birthright," said Jacob. "Ok," said Esau, "I'm too hungry to worry about it." So, Esau sold his birthright to his younger brother Jacob for a plate of food.

Back in Bible days, the first-born child usually received the birthright. It is a special blessing given to them by their father. But on this occasion, Esau did not seem to care about his birthright.

The brothers' father Isaac was aging and starting to lose his eyesight. So, one day Isaac called for his first-born son Esau and told him to, "Go out and kill a deer, then cook it for me. After I eat it, I will give you a special blessing as your birthright. I want to do this before I die." Isaac did not know his wife Rebekah was standing nearby listening as he talked to Esau.

When Esau left his father's tent, Rebekah hurried to tell her younger son Jacob about her plan for the two of them to deceive Isaac. Rebekah loved Jacob much more than she loved Esau. Plus, she remembered what God told her when she was pregnant. He said, "your older son will serve your younger son." So, she wanted to make sure that Jacob got his father's special blessing. Instead of letting God work out His own purpose and plans, she took matters into her own hands. She was like a smooth operator by getting her son Jacob to help her trick her aging husband.

Jacob went out and killed two baby goats at the urging of his mother. She said, "I will cook the meat the way your father likes it! After he eats it, he will bless you instead of your brother!" "But mother," said Jacob, "Esau has hairy skin, and my skin is smooth. He might realize it's me." "Just listen to your mother," replied Rebekah! "Put on Esau's clothes, because they smell like the fields!" Rebekah then took some goat skin and wrapped it around Jacob's arm and neck, just in case Isaac touched him. Next, Jacob took the cooked meat to his father, deceiving him, since Isaac could not see very well.

When Isaac finished eating, he blessed his younger son Jacob. All the time he thought he was blessing Esau, his favorite son.

This is some of what he said to Jacob...

"May God send lots of rain for your crops. May you have lots of grain and grapes. May you have lots of servants. May you be master of your brothers. May your mother's son bow down to you Everyone who curses you will be cursed. Everyone who blesses you, will be blessed."

As soon as Jacob left his father's bedside, Esau walked in and said, "Father, I'm back." I have the cooked meat that you like. Deer that I hunted from the fields! Eat father, so that you may bless me! I did exactly what you told me to do!"

"Who are you," said Isaac? "It is Esau, your first-born son." "What!" said Isaac, as his body shook uncontrollably. "Then who was the person that just left here? That person fed me, and I gave him a special blessing!

Esau cried out, "Oh father, bless me, too!" "It was your brother," said Isaac. "He tricked me and took your blessing!"

"No wonder they call him Jacob!" First, he tricked me out of my birthright; and now he has stolen my blessing!" "Oh father don't you have a blessing for me, cried Esau?"

Isaac said, "I have made Jacob lord over you and your relatives. He will have many crops and many servants." Esau continued to cry and begged his father for a blessing! Isaac finally told him this:

"The land you live on will not be very fertile, with very little rain. You will serve your brother. But one day, you will stop hating him."

After listening to his Father, Esau was very angry! He said, "I'm going to kill Jacob!" When Rebekah heard what Esau was going to do, she sent for Jacob. "Jacob!" said Rebekah, "listen to your mother! Quickly, go to Haran and stay with my brother Laban until Esau forgets what you have done to him! Then I will send for you to come back home."

Before Jacob left for Haran, Isaac called him into his tent to give him another blessing. This is some of what he said to Jacob....

"Do not marry a Canaanite woman. Instead, go to Haran where your mother's people are living. Choose one of your Uncle Laban's daughters to marry. And may God Almighty bless you and make you into a great nation. And Isaac sent Jacob away to Haran.

Jacob left his father to start on his journey. That night when he slept, he dreamed of stairs stretching from earth to heaven. He also saw the angels of God walking up and down the stairs. At the very top of the stairs stood God talking to Jacob. He said this:

"I am the God of Abraham and the God of your father Isaac. I'm going to give you and your descendants this land that you are now on. Your descendants will be so many as the dust on the ground. They will spread all over this land. All nations on earth will be blessed through you and your descendants. No matter where you go, I will always watch over you. And I will bring you back to this land. I will not leave you until I have done what I have said."

When Jacob woke up, he said, "God is in this place." He then took the stone that he had for his head and poured oil on top of it. Jacob set the stone up as a pillar and he called the place Bethuel. Then Jacob said this: "If God protects me and gives me food and clothes and allows me to come to my father's house again in peace, then God will be my God. This stone that I have set up for a pillar will be God's house. And, whatever God gives me, I will give a tenth of it back to him."

Jacob went on to Paddan Aram, where he arrived in Haran. This is the place of his mother's people. Here he met his Uncle Laban, who had two daughters. Jacob became more acquainted with Laban's younger daughter, Rachel. She was very beautiful, and Jacob fell in love with her.

One day Laban came to Jacob and asked him, "What do you want as pay for working for me?" Jacob said, "I will serve you seven years to marry your daughter Rachel." Laban agreed.

After the seven years were up, Laban tricked Jacob. Instead of giving him Rachel, he gave Jacob his older daughter Leah. Of course, Jacob was angry and asked Laban, "Why did you trick me?" Laban said, "It is tradition that the older daughter marries first. Finish the Week of Celebration and then I will give you Rachel. But agree to work for me for seven more years." Jacob agreed and Laban gave him Rachel as well. So Jacob worked for Laban seven more years.

Jacob really loved Rachel but he did not give Leah a lot of attention. So God allowed her to be fertile and have many children. Both of Jacob's wives had maids and Jacob also had children from them.

After many years of working for his Uncle, God came to Jacob and told him to leave Laban and go back to his father's homeland. So Jacob obeyed God and gathered all that he owned and set out for Canaan.

Jacob's traveling was not easy. He had in his company women with children, flocks of sheep and goats and herds of cattle. Many of the animals had nursing babies. And with all of this, he was chased down by his Uncle Laban and several other men. Uncle Laban was also Jacob's father-in-law. Laban was angry because Jacob left without saying a word. Seven days after Jacob and his family left, Laban caught up with them.

"Why did you sneak off like that?" asked Laban. You did not allow me to say good-bye to my daughters and grandchildren." I could really hurt you! But your father's God spoke to me last night and said, 'Be careful that you speak neither good nor bad to Jacob.'" Jacob answered, "I was afraid to tell you I was leaving because I thought you might take your daughters away from me."

Jacob and Laban talked through the night. And early the next morning Laban kissed and blessed his daughters and grandchildren. He then left to go back to his home.

So Jacob continued to travel back to his father's homeland. He sent a message to his brother Esau to let him know he was returning. He hoped that he would have favor in his brother's sight.

But Jacob did not get a good response from his brother. According to Jacob's messengers, Esau had 400 men with him and headed towards Jacob and his family. Jacob was very afraid because he did not know what was on Esau's mind or what was in his heart. Jacob quickly divided all of his possessions and family members into two groups. In case his brother attacked the family, at least one group would be able to escape.

Jacob began praying to God. "Deliver me from my brother's hand. I am afraid he will attack me and the mothers and my children. Lord you promised to increase my descendants like the sand, too many to count."

Later, Jacob wrestled with a man all night until daylight. This man could not stop Jacob. So the man struck Jacob on his hip and knocked it out of the joint socket. The man asked Jacob to let him go. But, Jacob said, "No! Not until you bless me!" The man said, "What is your name?" "My name is Jacob." "The man said, "Not anymore. Now you will be called Israel, because you have struggled with God and man, and you have won."

Jacob did not know who the man was. But the man blessed Jacob there. Jacob named that place Peniel, which means "I have seen God face to face and I am still alive."

That same day, Esau and his four hundred men traveled towards Jacob. Jacob still did not know how his brother would react. To his surprise, Esau ran to Jacob and kissed and hugged him. They both cried together! Then Jacob's family also came and bowed before Esau. The brothers socialized with each other for a while. Then it was time for them to continue back on their journeys. Each went their separate ways.

One day God came to Jacob and told him to move to Bethel. He said, "Settle there and build an altar to worship Me. I am the God who came to you when you ran from your brother." Jacob then told his whole household to get rid of their idols, take a bath, and put on clean clothes. Jacob said, "We will go up to Bethel where I will build an altar to God."

When Jacob and his household traveled through the towns of Canaan, the people who lived there were afraid of them. God had put fear in them so that they would not come after Jacob.

Another time God came to Jacob saying, "I am God Almighty, be fruitful and multiply. Kings will come from your descendants. I will give you the land that I gave your father Isaac and your grandfather Abraham."

While on their travels from Bethel to Ephrath, Jacob's wife Rachel died while giving birth to his last son. She named him Ben-Oni, but Jacob changed his name to Benjamin.

After many years of not seeing his father Isaac, Jacob was now in his presence. Isaac was living in the city of Hebron. But Isaac soon died at the age of 180 years old. Jacob and his brother Esau buried him.

Jacob suffered a few trials before his purpose was accomplished. He transformed from a con man or trickster into an obedient man. As a con man, he thought he could get what he wanted by tricking his brother and father. This brought Jacob much heartache. He had no choice but to leave his homeland because his angry brother Esau wanted to kill him. He soon found himself living around and working for his Uncle Laban, who was also a con man. Remember how he tricked Jacob into working another seven years for Rachel? But soon Jacob matured. He became an obedient man who trusted God for everything.

Proverbs 20:7 says, "The fair man walks in his integrity; His children are blessed after him." Just as his fathers before him, Jacob was called by God to be a Father of Many Nations. God blessed Jacob with much wealth. He also gave Jacob twelve sons and one daughter. And in the middle of Jacob's trials, God changed his name to Israel. His sons became the Twelve Tribes of Israel. The Israelites became a large nation, just as God said they would.

# Special Feature

**Names of Jacob's Thirteen Children and Their Mothers:**

| Children | Mothers |
|----------|---------|
| Reuben | Leah |
| Simeon | Leah |
| Levi | Leah |
| Judah | Leah |
| Dan | Rachel's maid, Bilhah |
| Naphtali | Rachel's maid, Bilhah |
| Gad | Leah's maid, Zilpah |
| Asher | Leah's maid, Zilpah |
| Issachar | Leah |
| Zebulun | Leah |
| Dinah | Leah |
| Joseph | Rachel |
| Benjamin | Rachel |

# Scripture References

Genesis 25: 21-34
Genesis 27: 1-45
Genesis 28: 1-5
Genesis 28: 10-22
Genesis 29: 1-35
Genesis 31: 3,17-18
Genesis 31: 22-29, 31, 55
Genesis 32: 3-31
Genesis 33: 1-11, 16-17
Genesis 35: 1-5

Genesis 35: 9-12
Genesis 35: 16, 18
Genesis 35: 27-29

## **Chapter Review**

1. How were the twin brothers different in their personalities?

2. How did Rebekah and Jacob trick his father, Isaac?

3. What kind of blessing did Isaac give his son, Jacob?

4. What did Jacob dream about when he journeyed from his father's house?

5. Why was Jacob afraid to tell his father-in-law that he was leaving?

6. Why was Jacob's name changed from Jacob to Israel?

7. Jacob transformed from a con man into what kind of man?

# 4

# Joseph

## Words to Know

**Accompany:** To go somewhere with another person.

**Assault:** To carry out a physical attack on someone or something.

**Baker:** A person who makes homemade bread, cakes, pies, and cookies.

**Beer-Sheba:** A place found in Canaan.

**Butler:** A person who runs another person's household.

**Convince:** To persuade another to believe as you do.

**Cupbearer:** A person who tastes food and drinks before the King does in order to make sure it is safe to eat.

**Curious:** When a person really wants to know something.

**Defeated:** Having been beaten in a battle or other contest.

**Embalmed:** To put a substance into a dead body so it won't decay and smell.

**Famine:** Very little food to eat.

**Good Fortune:** When only good things happen to a person or people.

**Goshen:** A place in Egypt that has good land.

**Governor:** Person in charge of administering and enforcing the laws of the land or territory.

**Grains:** Wheat, corn, or oats used for food.

**Harvest:** To pick crops that are ready to use for food.

**Hospitality:** Treating your visitor and guest very nice or making them feel welcome.

**Interpret:** To explain the meaning of something.

**Jehovah:** Another name for the God of Israel.

**Nile River:** The longest river in the world located in Africa.

**Observe:** To look at someone or something more closely.

**Occupation:** A job to make money to care for one's self and family.

**Palace:** A beautiful, large home.

**Patriarch:** The Head of his family.

**Pharaoh:** The King of Egypt.

**Plenty:** A lot of something.

**Portray:** To show or describe something or someone.

| | |
|---|---|
| **Priest:** | Men in the Bible who conduct or handle special ceremonies. |
| **Prison:** | A place of confinement or a large jail. |
| **Prosper:** | To increase in good health, strength, and riches. |
| **Prostrate:** | Face down lying on the ground or floor. |
| **Rape:** | Sexual intercourse by force. |
| **Rebuke:** | To express strong disapproval. |
| **Restore:** | To put back in the original position. |
| **Siblings:** | Brothers and sisters. |
| **Slave:** | A person who is the property of another and is forced to obey them. |
| **Stalk:** | When a person follows and watches you. |
| **Storehouse:** | A building to store things in. |
| **Survey:** | To carefully look at an area of land. |
| **Victories:** | To win or be successful at something. |

# 4

# Joseph
## Favorite Son of Israel

*A man who went from riches to rags and back again.
He also became second in command of Egypt.*

Joseph was born into a very wealthy family of twelve siblings. Only one other child would be born sometime after him. His father, Israel, was the patriarch of this large family. Israel was very happy to have another baby son. He loved this son above his other children because this son was born in Israel's old age. Rachael was the mother, and the wife that Israel truly loved. Rachael was also very happy, because she finally had her very own baby. She named the baby Joseph, which means, "May Jehovah give increase."

When Joseph was a teenager, his father Israel made him a special coat of many colors. The other older brothers were jealous. Their father had never given any of them such a gift. They also did not like Joseph because he once gave their father a bad report of them.

The brothers called Joseph the dreamer because Joseph would dream of them and share with them what those dreams were about. He once dreamed of his brother's sheaves of grain bowing down to his sheave of grain. Another time he dreamed that the sun, moon and eleven stars bowed down to him. When Joseph told his father Israel, he rebuked him. Israel also said, "Will your mother and I and your brothers actually bow to the ground before you?"

One day while the brothers were out in the field with the flock, they saw Joseph walking towards them. One of them said, "Here comes the dreamer! Let's kill him and throw him in a pit! We will tell father that he was eaten by a wild animal!" But Reuben the eldest brother convinced them not to kill him. "Let's just put him in this pit, so his blood won't be on our hands." Reuben thought he would come back later and pull Joseph out of the pit, then take him home to his father. But while Reuben was away, the rest of the brothers pulled Joseph out of the pit and took his coat of many colors off of him. Then, they sold Joseph to some Midianite traders who were traveling through the area.

When Reuben returned, he was sad and frustrated to see that Joseph was gone. His brothers told him what they had done. So they all decided to kill a goat and dip Joseph's coat in the goat's blood. They took the coat to their father and said, "We found this coat; could it be your son's?" Israel said, "It is my son's! A wild animal has torn him to pieces!" Israel was very sad and cried a lot. He grieved much for his son. All of his children tried to comfort him, but he would not be comforted. He said, "I will go to my grave, mourning my son Joseph."

By this time, Joseph was with the Midianites traveling to Egypt. When they arrived there, the Midianites sold Joseph as a slave to a man named Potiphar. This man was a captain of the guard for the Pharaoh of Egypt.

Joseph was a young man of about seventeen, separated from his family. He was now living in a foreign land. His parents must have taught him well, because people could see he was faithful to the Lord. Even his boss, Potiphar, could see that God was with him. Potiphar let Joseph live in his house. He also gave Joseph charge over his household plus everything that he owned. Potiphar was blessed in his house and in his fields because of Joseph.

Potiphar's wife saw how handsome and well-built Joseph was and she began to observe him often. One day in passing she said to Joseph, "Come lie down with me." "No!" said Joseph. "I will not do that! Your husband trusts me! Plus, I cannot sin against God!" So Potiphar's wife grabbed Joseph! But when he broke away from her, his jacket came off and was left in her hands.

As Joseph ran away from her, she started screaming! The other workers ran to her to see what happened. She did not tell the workers the truth. Instead, she said that Joseph tried to rape her. When her husband Potiphar came home, she told him the same thing. She also said, "Here is his jacket that he left behind." Even though this was not true, Potiphar was angry and he put Joseph in prison.

But God was still with Joseph while in prison. The chief prison guard trusted Joseph and put him in charge of the prisoners. God allowed Joseph to prosper. The chief guard did not have to check up on him.

Eight years later, the Pharaoh (King of Egypt) put two of his officials in prison. They were his chief butler and his chief baker. This was the same prison that Joseph was in. Joseph was in charge of them as well. One morning, Joseph noticed both of their faces. He said, "Why do you look so sad to-day?" Both men said they had dreams the night before! But neither could understand or explain their dreams.

With God's help Joseph interpreted their dreams. The butler had a good interpretation of his dream. Joseph told him that in three days, Pharaoh would give him his job back. "Remember me," said Joseph. "Tell the Pharaoh to get me out of here because I have done nothing wrong."

The baker did not have a good interpretation of his dream. Joseph told him, "In three days, Pharaoh will kill you."

Sure enough, three days later the Pharaoh celebrated his birthday. All of his servants were there. During this time, he restored the chief butler. But he killed the chief baker. And the chief butler forgot about Joseph.

Two more years passed, and Joseph was still in prison. About this same time, Pharaoh had two dreams that he could not interpret. After each dream, he woke up with a troubled mind. So Pharaoh sent for all the magicians and wise men of Egypt. They listened to Pharaoh's dreams, but they could not interpret them. Then Pharaoh's Chief Butler remembered Joseph. "Oh Pharaoh," said the butler. "I for-got about this young man, a Hebrew, that I met in prison!" "His name is Joseph!" "When I and your Chief Baker were in prison, he interpreted the dreams we had. And just as he said, the thing came true in our lives." "You restored me as Chief Butler and you killed the Chief Baker." So the Pharaoh sent for Joseph.

Joseph shaved and changed his clothes. He was then taken to the Pharaoh. "I have heard that you interpret dreams," Pharaoh said to Joseph. "It's really not me, but God who interprets dreams," said Joseph. Pharaoh went on to tell Joseph about his dreams. He said, "As I stood near the Nile River, I saw seven fat and pretty cows come out of the river. They ate the grass along the river. Then seven more cows came out of the river. But these cows were skinny and ugly. Now these skinny cows ate up the fat cows, and they were still skinny. Then I woke up. When I went back to sleep, I had another dream. I saw seven heads of grain on one stalk. The heads were stout and full. And then from the same stalk came seven more heads of grain. But these seven heads were all dried up. The dried heads of grain swallowed the seven full heads."

"Both dreams have the same meaning," said Joseph. "The seven fat cows and the seven full heads of grain means seven years of plenty. The seven skinny cows and the seven dried up heads of grain means seven years of famine."

Joseph spoke this to Pharaoh: "God will allow all of this to come about soon. I recommend that you find a wise man and put him in charge of Egypt. Also, appoint others to help. Food gathered during the years of plenty should be stored and used during the years of famine."

Joseph's words pleased the Pharaoh. He told his officials that Joseph was filled with the spirit of God. Then Pharaoh looked at Joseph and said, "God showed you my dreams, so you are the wisest man here. I am putting you in charge of the whole land of Egypt." While talking to Joseph, Pharaoh took off his ring and placed it on Joseph's finger. Pharaoh also dressed him in nice clothes and put a gold chain around his neck. Joseph was given a chariot with the position of second-in-command of Egypt. Pharaoh named Joseph Zaphnath-Paaneah and gave him a wife named Asenath. So Joseph went out and surveyed all the land of Egypt. He was thirty years old at the time.

The land of Egypt was very fertile during the seven years of plenty. Joseph gathered much grain as the sand on the beach. He stored up the overflow of grain in the different cities. The storehouses were too full to measure.

Joseph and his wife had two sons born during the seven years of plenty. He named his first son Manasseh, meaning "God made me forget my problems and my father's family." Joseph named his second son Ephraim, meaning "God made me fruitful in this land where I suffered."

After the seven years of plenty, the seven years of famine started. Different areas around Egypt, and Egypt as well were experiencing crop failures. People were starving and crying to Pharaoh for food. Pharaoh said, "Go to Joseph and do what he tells you to do. So Joseph opened the store houses where the extra grain was stored. He sold grain to the Egyptians and people from other countries, for the famine was all over the earth.

The famine was also in Canaan. This is the land where Joseph's father and brothers were living. Israel (which is Jacob's new name) said to his sons, "Why are you all hanging around here looking at each other? People say there is corn in Egypt! Get down there and buy us some so that we may live and not die!" Israel sent ten of his sons down to Egypt. He did not let his younger son Benjamin go because he was afraid something bad might happen to him.

When Joseph's ten brothers arrived in Egypt, they bowed down to the governor who was over the land. They did not know that the governor was their brother Joseph. However, Joseph recognized them right away. But he did not let himself be known to them. Joseph spoke to them roughly. He said, "You are all spies! You came to see where our weaknesses are in the land!" "No! My lord, we came to buy food," said one of the men. "We are brothers of one man, not spies! We are from Canaan. Our father is there now with our younger brother. One of our brothers has died." "I still say you are spies," said Joseph! "If you are not spies, then prove it to me. One of you go back to Canaan and get your brother. The rest of you will wait here in prison," said Joseph.

The brothers were put in prison for three days. Then Joseph went to them and said, "I will keep one of you here in prison. The rest of you may take food home to your families. But come back with your younger brother."

The brothers talked among themselves saying, "We treated our brother Joseph badly! When the traders bought and took him away, we saw the hurt and anguish on Joseph's face! That's why this is happening to us!" Then Reuben said, "I told you all not to do it, but nooo, you did not listen! Now we are going to die because we killed our brother!" The brothers did not know that Joseph understood what they were saying. Joseph turned away, left the room and cried! When he came back, he took Simeon and tied him up. Joseph would keep him as a hostage in prison until the other brothers returned.

Joseph was curious to see what type of men his brothers were now. So, he ordered that their sacks be filled with corn along with the return of their money. Joseph also gave the brothers extra grain for their journey. But the brothers did not know that Joseph had done this.

So, the brothers set out for home, back to Canaan. When they stopped to rest, one of the brothers opened his sack. He was surprised to see that the money to be paid for the grain was returned to him. All the brothers were afraid. One of them said, "What has God done to us?"

Finally, the brothers arrived in Canaan. They told their father everything that happened in Egypt. They also told him that the governor over the land talked roughly to them. "He said bring your younger brother back. This will prove to me that you are not spies."

While talking with their father, they opened their sacks. Each brother had his money returned back to him. This frightened them and their father.

Israel cried to his sons, "You have deprived me of my children! Joseph is gone! Simeon is gone! And now you want to take Benjamin away from me!" Then Reuben, the older brother, said, "You may kill my two sons if I do not bring him back. Israel said, "Oh no! I will not let Benjamin go."

The famine was still going on all around the land. Soon all the grain was gone. So Jacob told his sons to go back to Egypt and buy some more grain. Judah spoke up, "Remember father, the Governor will not even see us unless we have our younger brother with us." "Why did you tell him you had another brother," asked Israel. Then the brothers replied, "The man asked if we had any other brothers." Judah told his father that he would take full responsibility for Benjamin.

Israel their father agreed to let Benjamin go. "But I want you all to fill your sacks with the very best things we have here. Give them to the man in charge as gifts. Be sure to take with you some balm, honey, spices, myrrh, pistachio nuts, and almonds. Also, take double the money that you found in your sacks, maybe it was mistakenly put back. May God Almighty have mercy on you and return both Simeon and Benjamin." Israel said sadly, "If I do not see my sons again, then so be it."

The brothers loaded up the goods and went down to Egypt. When they arrived, Joseph could see that Benjamin was with them. Joseph said to the servant in charge of his house, "Take the men to my house. Also kill an animal and prepare a meal. I will have lunch with them today."

So the servant took the men to Joseph's palace. They told the servant that their money was returned to them. But the servant said, "Do not worry about it. Maybe the God of your fathers gave the money back to you. I already have the money that you paid for the grain." The servant was very kind to the brothers. He had their animals fed and gave them water to wash their feet. The servant also brought Simeon out to them.

When Joseph came home, the brothers presented him with all the gifts they brought. The brothers bowed low before him. Joseph said, "How is your father doing?" One brother said, "Your servant, our father, is alive and doing well." Then the brothers bowed down again and prostrated themselves before Joseph. When Joseph looked around and saw Benjamin, he said, "Is this your younger brother whom you told me about? May God be gracious to you, my son." Joseph was emotional and left the room quickly! He went to another room to cry! After washing his face, he came back with the brothers and said, "Let the food be served."

Everyone was divided when they sat down to eat. Joseph sat by himself. The brothers sat together by themselves and the Egyptians sat by themselves. The brothers were surprised that they had been seated according to their ages. Benjamin, the youngest brother, was given five times more food than the others. Nevertheless, they all ate, drank and enjoyed themselves.

Now it was time for the brothers to leave. So, Joseph had his chief servant load up their sacks with as much grain as they could carry. Joseph said, "Give each man his money back. And put my silver cup in the younger man's sack."

After the men left to journey home, Joseph told his servant to go after them. He said, "When you catch them, say why did you steal my master's silver cup?" So, Joseph's servant did as he was told. The brothers were shocked that they had been accused falsely. They said, "We did not steal from your master. But if you find it among us, that person should die and the rest of us should be taken as slaves." Joseph's servant agreed with the brothers.

The servant searched all the sacks and found the silver cup in Benjamin's sack. The brothers tore their clothes because they were so sad.

All the brothers were taken back to Joseph's house. When they saw him, they bowed down low before him. Joseph spoke harshly, "Why have you done this? Did you not know that I would find out?" So, Judah said, "What can we say? How can we prove we are innocent? God is punishing us for our sins. Lord, we will all be your slaves." Joseph said, "No, only the man who stole the cup will be my slave. I will let the rest of you go home."

Judah came closer to Joseph and said, "My Lord, may I say something. But please do not get angry with me, for I know you are equal to Pharaoh. Sir, I cannot go back home without my father's son! If my father sees that his youngest son is not with us, he will die! Please sir, let me take his place! I will be your slave instead! Let the lad return with his brothers!"

Joseph cried out loud to his servants in the room, "Get out all of you!" Joseph cried so loud that he could be heard by all the people in the house! While Joseph was left alone with his brothers, he said, "I am Joseph. Is my father still alive? The brothers did not say a word. They were shocked and afraid. Then Joseph said, "Come closer to me!" So the brothers came closer. "I am Joseph, your brother! The one you sold into Egypt! Do not be angry with yourselves! God had sent me ahead of you, to keep you and your family alive! For you will become a great nation! God made me an adviser to Pharaoh. Pharaoh chose me to manage his household. He also made me ruler over all the land of Egypt: second-in-command next to him."

Joseph told his brothers to go back home quickly. He said, "Tell my father to come down to Egypt so that I may take care of you all. For there are still five more years of famine. The whole family with the flocks and herds may live in Goshen. You will be near me. Be sure to tell my father of all my glory in Egypt." Then Joseph hugged his younger brother and cried. And Benjamin cried as well. Joseph also hugged the rest of his brothers. Everybody was filled with joy and talked freely.

Pharaoh and all of his servants were pleased when they heard Joseph's brothers were there from Canaan. Pharaoh said to Joseph, "Tell your brothers to go get their families and bring them to Egypt. I will give them the best land in Egypt. They shall take wagons from here for their wives and children to ride in."

Before Joseph sent his brothers off, he made sure they had plenty of goods including:

- enough food for the journey back to Canaan.
- a new set of clothes for each older brother.
- five changes of new clothes and three hundred pieces of silver, just for Benjamin.
- ten donkeys loaded with good things of Egypt.
- ten donkeys loaded with grain and other food.

As the brothers left, Joseph yelled out to them, "Do not argue with each other!"

The brothers arrived back in Canaan and yelled out to their father. "Joseph is still alive! He is governor over all the land of Egypt! He wants the whole family to move to Egypt, for there are five more years of famine left! He said he will take care of us!" At first, Israel would not believe what they were saying. But when he saw the wagons and all the rest of the goods, his mind was refreshed. Israel said, "Joseph is alive! I will go see my son before I die!

So Israel, with his whole family, flocks, and herds, journeyed towards Egypt. On the way, they stopped in Beer-sheba and Israel offered sacrifices to God. That night, God spoke to Israel in a vision. He said, "Jacob! Jacob! I am the God of your father Isaac! Do not be afraid to go down to Egypt, for I will be with you. I will make you a great nation. You will die in Egypt, but your descendants will come back and live in Canaan." So Israel was comforted and encouraged. He continued his journey to Egypt.

When Joseph met his father Israel in Goshen, they hugged each other and cried for a while. Israel told Joseph, "Now let me die, for I have seen you, and you are alive!"

Joseph and five of his brothers went to see the Pharaoh. Joseph said, "My father is here, in the land of Goshen, with the whole family, flocks and herds." The Pharaoh asked the brothers what their occupation was. They said, "We and our fathers are shepherds. We pray that you let us (your servants) live in the land of Goshen. "Okay," said the Pharaoh. "This is the best land in Egypt. Also, if you know of any men who are able, put them in charge of my cattle."

When Joseph brought his father to see Pharaoh, Israel blessed the Pharaoh. The Pharaoh asked Israel, "How old are you?" "I have lived one hundred and thirty hard years," said Israel. "But some of my ancestors lived much longer than I have." And Israel blessed Pharaoh one more time before he left.

So Joseph gave his family the best land in Egypt as Pharaoh commanded. And Joseph provided all of his father's household with bread. At that time, there was no bread in the land because the famine was so severe.

Joseph had plenty of grain in the storehouses. The storehouses were in different cities throughout Egypt. People came from Canaan and from all over Egypt looking for bread. Joseph sold them grain for money and he put the money into Pharaoh's house. When the people ran out of money, he sold them grain for their cattle and their other animals. Soon their animals were gone. The people were so desperate for food that they were willing to sell their land and become slaves to Pharaoh. So, Joseph bought the people and their land. Through this exchange they would get seed to plant and work the land for free. The people were allowed to keep four-fifths of the crops harvested, and one-fifths of the crops would go to Pharaoh. So the Pharaoh owned all the land in Egypt except for the priest's land.

Now Israel and his descendants lived in the very fertile land of Goshen. While there, they prospered greatly.

One day, Israel called for Joseph. He said, "Please promise me that you will not bury me here in Egypt. Instead, take me up to Canaan and bury me with my fathers at Hebron in the cave of Machpelah. When Joseph promised his father that he would do it, Israel bowed in worship.

A short while later, Joseph got word that his father was sick. So Joseph and his sons, Manasseh and Ephraim, went to visit Israel. At that time, Israel blessed Joseph's two sons. Israel also said, "I am dying, but God will take you back to the land of your fathers."

Right before Israel died, he called for the rest of his sons. They all gathered around his bed. Then, he told each of them what will happen to them and their descendants in the coming future. And Israel blessed all of his sons and told them where he wanted to be buried. When Israel finished talking to his sons, he died. Joseph fell on his father's face and cried. He also kissed him. Israel was one-hundred and forty seven years old.

Joseph had his father embalmed. And when the days of mourning were over, Pharaoh allowed Joseph and his family members to go up to Canaan to bury Israel. Some of the Egyptians went with Joseph and his family to Canaan to bury Israel.

Now that their father was dead, the brothers were afraid that Joseph would get revenge on them. So, they went to Joseph and bowed down before him and said, "We are your slaves." Joseph said, "Do not be afraid, for I am not God. You meant evil against me, but God turned it to good. He did this so that many would be saved from starvation. I will continue to take care of you and your families." Joseph comforted his brothers by speaking kind words to them.

Some years later, Joseph said to his brothers, "I am about to die, but God will take you out of Egypt. He will take you to the land (Canaan) that he promised to Abraham, Isaac, and Israel. When this happens, please take my bones with you." Joseph lived to be one-hundred and ten years old. And in that time, he saw and spent time with his son's grandchildren.

Joseph was an amazing man. He was a man of principles and integrity. He had the spirit of the living God in him because his parents taught him to love and obey God. Even when Joseph was sold away from his family and homeland, he stayed faithful to God. He willingly forgave his brothers for their cruelty. "And we know that all things work for good to those who love the Lord and who are called according to his purpose," says Romans 8:28. Joseph was trusted to run another man's household. He was trusted to be in charge of prisoners. With God's help, he was trusted to interpret dreams. Pharaoh, the King of Egypt, trusted Joseph to manage the crops in times of plenty, and during the time of famine. Joseph managed them very well. He was able to gather wealth for the Pharaoh by selling grain to the people who were out of food.

Clearly, God had a special purpose for Joseph. But first he would experience some defeats and many victories. These defeats and victories prepared Joseph to do what he was born for: to save his family and many others from starvation.

# Special Feature

## *Joseph's Struggles*

- His older brothers hated him.

- At seventeen, his jealous brothers threw him in a pit. Then they sold him to Midianite traders.

- He was taken to Egypt and sold into slavery.

- Potiphar's wife accused him of trying to lie down with her. Potiphar threw him into prison.

- He was left in prison for ten years. But he was innocent. One inmate forgot about Joseph.

## *Joseph's Victories*

- He was born to wealthy parents who loved him very much.

- He was Israel's favorite child. Israel gave Joseph a coat of many different colors.

- Potiphar trusted Joseph and allowed him to run his household.

- While in prison, the chief jailer trusted Joseph and allowed him to be in charge of the prisoners.

- With God's help, he was able to interpret two of his inmate's dreams.

- The inmate remembered Joseph and told Pharaoh about him. He interpreted Pharaoh's dreams.

- Pharaoh, the King of Egypt, said that Joseph was filled with the spirit of God. The King liked and trusted the advice that Joseph gave him, concerning his dreams. So, Pharaoh promoted Joseph to second-in-command, over all the land of Egypt. Joseph was only thirty years old at the time.

- Pharaoh gave Joseph a wife and they were blessed with two sons.

- He became a good manager of crops during the time of plenty and the time of famine.

- He forgave his brothers and helped save his family from starvation. He moved the whole family near him, down in Egypt. They lived in the very fertile area of Goshen.

- Before Joseph's father died, he pronounced a blessing upon Joseph's two sons. Their names were Manasseh and Ephraim.

# Scripture References

Genesis 37: 9-36
Genesis 39: 1-23
Genesis 40: 1-23
Genesis 41: 1-57
Genesis 42: 1-38
Genesis 43: 1-34
Genesis 44: 1-34
Genesis 45: 1-28
Genesis 46: 1-4
Genesis 46: 29-30
Genesis 47: 1-31

Genesis 48: 1, 20, 21
Genesis 49: 1, 28-29, 33
Genesis 50: 1, 2, 4, 7, 15, 18-26

# Chapter Review

1. Why did Joseph's father make him a coat of many colors?

2. Why did Joseph's brothers throw him into a pit, and then sell him to Midianite traders?

3. Where was Potiphar blessed because of Joseph?

4. Why did Joseph shave and change his clothes?

5. How many of Pharaoh's dreams did Joseph interpret?

6. What came after seven years of plenty?

7. Do you think this Pharaoh was a good man? If yes, why?

# 5

# Moses

## Words to Know

**Accomplish:**    The act of a person finishing a task.

**Aggressive:**    A very intense effort at something.

**Bulrushes:**    Green plants that can grow up to ten feet in wet and muddy shallow water.

**Children of Israel:**    People who were descendants of Jacob (now called Israel).

**Cruel:**    The act of causing pain and suffering to others.

**Defects:**    Something or someone not perfect because of a flaw or blemish.

**Deliverer:**    A person who rescues others.

**Goshen:**    A place in Egypt where the children of Israel lived.

**Harsh:**    Something done or said in a hard or a rough way.

**Hebrew:**    Another name for the children of Israel.

| | |
|---|---|
| **Hired:** | Paying a person for a particular job. |
| **Israelites:** | A nation of people who came from Jacob. |
| **Launch:** | To set off or send off; to start something new. |
| **Mature:** | A person who is accountable for their actions and able to make responsible decisions. |
| **Midwife:** | Women who help other women in the birth of their babies. |
| **"Milk and Honey":** | Symbolizes something good or something in abundance. |
| **Miracles:** | Events that do not happen in a natural way or something good which cannot be explained. |
| **Multiply:** | To increase something greatly in number or quantity. |
| **Patriarch:** | A man who is the head of his family. |
| **Pillar of cloud:** | Used to guide the children of Israel through the desert during the day when they left Egypt. |
| **Pillar of Fire:** | Used to guide the children of Israel through the desert during the night when they left Egypt. |
| **Pitch:** | A sticky and gummy substance also known as tar or a liquid that comes from coal, wood or petroleum. |
| **Prosper:** | To increase in good health, strength, and riches. |
| **Rescue:** | To save someone from harm and danger or to set a person or animal free. |

| | |
|---|---|
| **Rod/Staff:** | A long stick used by shepherds to care for sheep and goats. |
| **Serpent:** | A large snake. |
| **Shepherd:** | A person who takes care of sheep. |
| **Slave:** | A person who is the property of another and is forced to obey them. |
| **Slave Master:** | A person who is in charge of slaves; they tell the slaves what to do. |
| **Slime:** | A substance like soft mud or clay. |
| **Sorcerers/Magicians:** | People who practice witchcraft or magic tricks. |
| **Sorrows:** | Very sad feelings over the loss of someone or something that is loved. |
| **Strike:** | To hit someone or something with force. |
| **Throne:** | A chair for a very important person to sit on. |
| **Tribe:** | A group of families or communities living together. |
| **Unleavened Bread:** | A flat bread that does not have rising agents such as yeast or baking powder. |
| **Wilderness:** | A place overgrown with lots of trees and plants or a natural place not touched by humans. |
| **Worship:** | To give honor and reverence to God or to another person. |

# 5

## Moses
### Deliverer of God's People

Thehe Israelites came from the twelve sons of Jacob. However, it's amazing how the Israelite people got their name. One night, Jacob wrestled with a man whom he did not know. They wrestled until daylight, but Jacob refused to let the man go. Jacob said, "I will not let you go until you bless me." The man asked, "What is your name?" "I am Jacob." "Not anymore," said the man. "Now you will be called Israel, because you have struggled with God and man and you have won."

Israel's son Joseph was already living in Egypt. It was through Joseph that Israel's whole family came to live in Egypt as well. Joseph helped save them from starvation. For many years, the Israelites lived well in Egypt, in the land of Goshen. They had become a very large nation. This is just what God promised the three Patriarchs, that they would be **Fathers of Many Nations**. For years while in Egypt, the Israelites multiplied, prospered, and lived in good health. The Pharaoh of that time knew Joseph and was kind to his family. But many years had passed since those good old days and new Pharaohs came to the throne.

These Pharaohs did not know Joseph's family and all the work Joseph did for Egypt. The Israelites were multiplying so much that the king feared them. He said, "There are so many Israelites in the land. If war breaks out, they might join with another nation and overtake us. We must do something about these people."

So the Egyptians made slaves out of the Israelites. Harsh and cruel slave masters were put over them. The slaves were forced to build the cities of Pithom and Rameses for the Pharaoh. It seems as though the harder the Egyptians were to the Israelites, the more the Israelites multiplied. Soon the Pharaoh, King of Egypt told the midwives this:

"When you help the Israelite women give birth, I want you to kill all the boys." But the two midwives, Shiphrah and Puah, refused to obey the king. They told the king that,

"Israelite women have their babies fast before we can get there." And because of this, God blessed the midwives with their own families and the Israelites continued to multiply. So, the Pharaoh told his people to throw all newborn Israelite boys into the Nile River.

It was during this time that a baby boy was born to Amram and Jochebed, both from the tribe of Levi. The baby's mother Jochebed was able to hide her baby for three months. But as the baby grew bigger and became noisier, she knew she needed to be more aggressive in order to keep her baby safe. So she gathered bulrushes near the river and used them to make a basket. She put slime and pitch on and around the basket to keep water from coming in. Then she laid her baby in the basket and placed it in the water near the riverbank between the long bulrushes. The baby's older sister was not too far away, watching to see what would happen.

Pharaoh's daughter had been bathing nearby when she noticed the basket. So she sent one of her maids to get it for her. When she opened it, the baby was crying. And she had compassion for him. She said, "This is one of the Israelites children." Then the baby's sister who came closer said, "Shall I go and get one of the Israelite women to nurse the baby? "Yes," said Pharaoh's daughter. The baby's sister ran home and got her and the baby's mother and brought her to Pharaoh's daughter. She hired the woman to nurse the baby. When the child grew, the woman brought him back to Pharaoh's daughter and he became her son. She named him Moses because she drew him out of the water.

Even though Moses grew up around royalty, he knew he was an Israelite. One day, he went to Goshen where the Israelite slaves lived. While there, he saw an Egyptian strike an Israelite. So Moses looked around to make sure no one was watching and he killed that Egyptian, then hid his body in the sand. The very next day, he went back to Goshen and saw two Israelite slaves fighting. He did not like that. He said to the one who attacked first, "Why did you strike your brother like that?"

The man said, "Who made you prince and judge over us? Are you going to kill me like you did the Egyptian yesterday?" After hearing what the man said, Moses was scared that Pharaoh, the King of Egypt, would also find out that he killed an Egyptian.

Soon enough, Pharaoh did find out what Moses had done and wanted to kill him. But Moses ran away from Egypt and lived in the land of Midian. He was forty years old at the time. The land of Midian was good for Moses because this was the place where he started to mature. While there, he rescued a group of seven sisters. They had drawn water from a well to give to their father's sheep. But shepherds came and drove them away. Moses, who was sitting near the well, saw the whole thing. So he sprang to his feet and stopped the shepherds. Then he gave the sisters sheep water to drink.

Moses spent forty years in the land of Midian. He became a shepherd and learned to take care of sheep. He married Zipporah, one of the seven sisters that he rescued. His wife's father was Jethro the Priest of Midian. Moses was blessed with two sons, Gershom and Eliezer.

Another spectacular thing that happened to Moses was when God spoke to him through a burning bush. One day, Moses was out with his father-in-law's sheep when he noticed a bush was on fire but did not burn up. So Moses went closer to it. Then he heard a voice say, "Moses, take off your shoes, for this is holy ground." And God said to Moses, "I am the God of Abraham, Isaac, and Jacob. I have seen my people suffering in Egypt. I have come to deliver them out of the Egyptians hands. I will bring them into a good land that flows with milk and honey. Moses, I will send you to deliver the children of Israel out of Egypt."

Moses knew that was God talking to him, but he was not sure if this was something he should do. He thought he was not good enough to do such an important work. So, he began to ask God questions.

## Statements and Questions Moses had for God
Who shall I say sent me? What if they don't believe me? God, I am not a good speaker.

## God's Responses
"Tell them 'I Am' has sent you. Perform miracles that I will show you. Who made man's mouth? Isn't it I? Go, I will help you as you talk. Plus, I will give you the words to say." God was angry with Moses. But He told Moses to take his brother Aaron with him because he is a good speaker and that He would be with both of them as they spoke.

So God answered all of Moses' questions and assured Moses that He would be with him. He told Moses that the people in Egypt who wanted to kill him were dead.

Moses went to his boss and father-in-law, Jethro. He said, "Let me go back to Egypt to see if my family members are still alive." "Go in peace," said Jethro. So Moses with his wife and two sons loaded a donkey and went to Egypt. He also had the rod of God in his hand.

God sent Moses' brother, Aaron, into the wilderness to meet Moses. After greeting each other, Moses told Aaron everything that God said they were to do. When they arrived in Egypt, the two brothers met with all the elders from the Israelite tribes. Aaron did most of the talking. He told the elders what God said to Moses. Then Moses performed the miracles God had shown him. One of the miracles was this: he laid his rod on the ground and the rod turned into a snake. When Moses picked up the snake by the tail, it turned back into a rod. All the elders worshipped God, because they were glad that He had seen their sorrows. At this time Moses was eighty years old and his brother Aaron was eighty-three years old.

Later, Moses and Aaron went to talk to Pharaoh and told him this, "The Lord God of Israel said, to let my people go to hold a feast to Me in the wilderness." "Who is the Lord? I do not know him, and I will not let Israel go," said Pharaoh.

That very same day, Pharaoh made it hard for the children of Israel. He ordered the cruel slave masters to refuse to give straw to the slaves to make bricks. Now, the slaves had to find their own straw, making their jobs even harder. The Israelite slaves were angry with Moses and Aaron. They said, "You made us look bad in front of the Pharaoh and his servants. Now, they probably think they have the right to kill us."

So, Moses went to God and said, "Lord, why are you treating the Israelite slaves this way? And why did you send me? After I talked to the Pharaoh, he became more evil toward the Israelites and You have not delivered them."

"Moses, soon you will see what I will do to Pharaoh," God said.

"With a strong hand, Pharaoh will let them go and he will drive them out of his country. For I am the Lord. I have heard the cries of the children of Israel."

Moses and Aaron went back to Pharaoh to tell him to let God's people go, but Pharaoh would not. So Aaron threw the rod in front of Pharaoh, just as God said. And the rod became a serpent. Then Pharaoh called in his sorcerers (Egyptian Magicians) to do the same thing. Their rods also became serpents. But Aaron's rod swallowed the rods of the magicians. And the Pharaoh still would not listen. So Moses and Aaron left.

Moses and Aaron came back several times to tell the Pharaoh that God said, "Let my people go." When Pharaoh refused, they announced a plague in Egypt. Sometimes, Pharaoh would say, "Tell God to take this plague away," or he would just say, "No, I will not let the Hebrews go." There were ten plagues God placed on the Egyptians.

**The first nine plagues:**

- The Nile River was turned into blood.
- Frogs covered the land of Egypt.
- There was an infestation of gnats.
- Flies swarmed throughout Egypt.
- Egypt's animals died (but not Israelites).
- Boils broke out on the Egyptians and their animals.
- Hailstorms destroyed crops, animals, and people.
- Locusts ate crops left over from the hailstorm.
- There was total darkness for three days (but not for the Hebrews).

Even after experiencing these nine plagues, the Pharaoh's heart was hardened and he still refused to let God's people go.

God told Moses that He had one more plague to bring upon the Egyptians. Then the Pharaoh would let the Israelites go. So Moses went back to Pharaoh and told him what God said.

"About midnight, I will go throughout Egypt and all the first born there will die. This will include the first born of Pharaoh, and the Egyptian slaves' first born. The first-born animals owned by the Egyptians will also die. There will be such a loud cry in Egypt, like never before or ever again! None of the Israelites will die, nor their animals. Then Pharaoh will know that God put a difference between the Egyptians and the Israelites!"

Again, God spoke to Moses and Aaron saying, "Tell the Israelites to pick out a perfect animal with no defects. The animal is to be a lamb or a goat male about one year old. The animal should be set apart from other animals on the tenth of the month. Then, the animal will be killed on the fourteenth day, in the evening. Take hyssop and dip it in the animals' blood and place the blood on the sides of the door post and at the top of the door post. Two families may share the meal if the families are small. The people shall not eat the meat raw or boiled. The animal must be roasted that night and eaten in a hurry with unleavened bread and bitter herbs. Whatever is left, burn it up and do not leave any for leftovers. Be fully dressed with shoes on and a staff in hand while eating because everyone will be leaving soon. This is the Lord's Passover. For I will pass throughout Egypt, killing all the first born of the Egyptian people and animals. But when I see the blood on the door post of the Israelites, I will pass over them and not harm those who are inside." God also told Moses and Aaron that this month will be a very special month. It will be the first month of the year from now on, and God's people should celebrate it from year to year.

Sometimes in the middle of the night, the Pharaoh called for Moses and Aaron. He told them, "Get out of the land of Egypt, and take everything you own with you, your people, and your animals." Before they left, God gave the Israelites favor in the sight of the Egyptians. When God's people asked for clothes, silver and gold jewels, the Egyptians gave it to them.

The Israelites lived in Egypt for 430 years. The first few years there, they lived in peace. It was sometime after Joseph died that the Israelites were made slaves. The whole time they were in Egypt, the Israelites multiplied into a very large nation, just as God said they would. The Israelites left Egypt with six hundred thousand men, plus women and children. They also had many flocks, herds, and cattle. Some of the people who left with the Israelites were Egyptians. Moses also took the bones of Joseph with him. For Joseph told the Israelites that "God will visit you, and you shall carry my bones away from here."

When the people left Egypt, they always had light to see where they were going. They were able to travel during the daytime and at night. For God had put a pillar of cloud in the day sky and pillar of fire in the night sky. God did not lead his people through the land of the Philistines, even though that was the shortest way. God did not want the Israelites to see war or return to Egypt. Instead, he led them the long way, towards the wilderness and the Red Sea.

Now Moses and the Israelites were camped near the Red Sea, where God had led them. When Pharaoh heard where they were, he and his army with chariots and horses came after them! For God made Pharaoh's heart hard, so as to show the Egyptians that God is Lord! The Israelites saw that the Egyptians were coming closer to them, and they were so afraid! And Moses said, "Do not be afraid. Stand still and see the salvation of the Lord! You will never see these Egyptians again."

God caused the pillar of cloud to turn dark for the Egyptians, so they could not see the Israelites. But for the Israelites, the pillar of cloud was still light, even in the dark. God told Moses to lift the rod and stretch his hands over the sea and divide it! The Lord pushed the sea back with a strong east wind all night! The Israelites were able to walk through the divided sea on dry ground! However, the Egyptians, with all their horses and chariots, chased after the Israelites through the divided sea! Soon, God allowed his chosen people to reach the other side of the sea! Moses did what God told him to do. He stretched out his hand again over the sea and the water came back in place, drowning all of those Egyptians! After witnessing this spectacular event, the Israelites reverently feared God. They also believed in God and his servant Moses. They all sang a special song to God. After this, the Children of Israel would go on to experience many more of God's mighty miracles as they traveled toward the promised land.

Moses was born at a dangerous time in Egypt's history, but it was the right time. Finally, God was ready to set his people free from slavery. And he chose Moses as the deliverer. When God calls us for a special purpose, we can be sure that God will give us just what we need to accomplish it. Of course, it helped that Moses put his trust in God. God had given Moses just the right attributes. He was courageous, patient, responsible, and he had empathy for others. These are characteristics needed to manage a large group of people. And Moses would manage a whole nation - the Children of Israel.

# Special Feature

**Some of the Mighty Miracles God Performed for the Children of Israel**

- God sent plagues on Egypt so that the Pharaoh would let God's people go.

- God placed a pillar of cloud in the day sky to lead the Israelites by day. He also placed a pillar of fire in the night sky to lead the people by night.

- God opened the Red Sea and allowed the Israelites to cross it on dry ground. Then He let the Egyptians drown in the Red Sea when they chased after the Israelites. Now, the Egyptians were no longer a threat to God's chosen people.

- God provided his people with clear, clean water to drink as they wandered through the wilderness.

- God fed the people with bread from the sky. The Israelites called it manna. (Manna was like coriander seed and white in color. This manna had the taste of bread and honey.)

- Moses raised his hands and God allowed the Israelites to conquer the Amalekites in battle.

- God gave Moses two tablets of stone with the Ten Commandments written on them by His own finger.

# Scripture References

Genesis 32: 24-28
Exodus 1: 8-22
Exodus 2: 1-22
Exodus 3: 1-8
Exodus 3: 10-14
Exodus 4: 1-7, 10-16, 18-20
Exodus 4: 27-31
Exodus 5: 1, 2, 6-7, 21-23
Exodus 6: 1, 2, 5
Exodus 7: 10-12
Exodus 11: 1, 4-7
Exodus 12: 1-51
Exodus 13: 10, 17-19, 20-22
Exodus 14: 1, 2, 4, 8, 10, 13, 16, 19-23, 28-31
Exodus 15: 1
Exodus 17: 9-13
Exodus 18: 3-4
Exodus 20: 1-16

# Chapter Review

1. Why did the Egyptians make slaves out of the Israelites?

2. What did Moses' mother put around the basket that she made for Moses?

3. Who was Moses' father-in-law and what was his position in Midian?

4. How old were Moses and Aaron when they first met with all the elders from the Israelite tribes?

5. Yes or No: did any of the Israelites animals die during the fifth plaque?

6. Where was the animal's blood supposed to be placed so that God would see it, and would pass over the Israelites and not harm them?

7. Why did God send Moses to Egypt?

# 6

# Elijah

## Words to Know

| | |
|---|---|
| **Anoint:** | To rub or put oil on someone, either for healing or other purposes. |
| **Ashtoreth:** | A false god. |
| **Baal:** | A false god. |
| **Brook:** | A small body of flowing water; a stream. |
| **Devoured:** | To completely destroy. |
| **False Prophets:** | Not prophets of God. |
| **Humility:** | Not proud of oneself or not arrogant. |
| **Idol:** | An image that someone worship as their god. |
| **Influence:** | Able to affect another person or thing. |
| **Liveliest:** | Very active and energetic, or full of life. |
| **Mantle:** | A sleeveless garment worn by prophets symbolizing God's call to serve Him. |

**Profound:** Hard to understand.

**Prophet:** A man called to deliver God's special messages to His people.

**Prophetess:** A woman called to deliver God's special messages to His people.

**Reveal:** To make plain or clearer.

**Significant:** Something or someone important.

**Stamina:** Extra strength and energy in one's body.

**Task:** Work to be done.

**Trench:** A narrow ditch in the ground.

**Whirlwind:** Air moving around very fast in a funnel shape.

**Widow:** A woman whose husband has died.

**Worship:** To bow down to, or show honor to God, or other gods.

# 6

## Elijah
### One of God's Greatest Prophets Who Was Born to Reveal the Word of God

From Genesis to Revelation, the Bible is filled with fascinating stories of prophets. They were born for very important tasks. They were to reveal the word of God by telling people what God wanted them to know. They would often tell the people to turn away from their sins and back to God. Sometimes prophets did not have a peaceful life because they were bound to speak God's truth. When kings and other high officials did not want to hear the truth, they tried to have the prophets killed. But God was always there to protect them. Prophets, such as Isaiah, Jeremiah, Daniel, and many other men and women found in the Bible all made a significant impact on the nation of Israel, but none more profound than Elijah, the Tishbite.

I think Elijah was one of God's liveliest prophet because he let God use him and do amazing things through him. God filled Elijah with courage, unselfishness, strong faith, patience, humor, plus super strength and stamina.

God called Elijah during the time when Ahab was King of Israel. Ahab was an evil king, married to Jezebel, who was more evil than he was. Jezebel influenced her husband into worshipping false gods, Baal, and other gods. King Ahab caused so many people to turn away from God and to idol worship. He brought out God's anger more than any other king before him. So, God sent Elijah with this strong message for King Ahab: "No dew or rain shall fall on the land, unless I say so." (In other words, there will be a drought.) A drought is not a comfortable thing to live through. It means very little water and food for both humans and animals.

Elijah showed courage while standing before the King, with such a powerful message. The King could have had his life taken away instantly. But God allowed Elijah to leave the palace unharmed.

Because Elijah's life was still in danger, God told him to hide near the brook, Cherith. Here he would drink water from the brook and eat food brought to him by ravens. God had commanded the ravens to feed him. And it was so. Each morning and evening, the ravens brought him bread and meat. Can you imagine eating breakfast and dinner given to you each day by birds? That's awesome! Eventually the brook dried up, because of no rain. So God told Elijah to go to Zarephath, where he commanded a woman to take care of him. This very poor woman was a widow who was raising her son alone.

When Elijah got there, he asked the woman for a piece of bread. She said, "I have no bread. I only have a little flour and oil, which I will use to bake me and my son's last meal. Then we will die." "Don't be afraid," said Elijah. "Bake me a little cake first, then go back and bake for you and your son. For the Lord God of Israel says you won't run out of flour and oil during this drought." The woman did as Elijah said.

As time passed, the woman's son died. When she told Elijah, he prayed to God and God brought the woman's son back to life. After this, the woman believed that Elijah was a man of God.

About three years later, God sent Elijah to tell King Ahab that it would rain soon. When the King saw Elijah, he falsely accused the prophet. He said, "You have brought disaster upon the nation of Israel." "No," said Elijah. "It is you and your father's house who have hurt Israel. You have done this by worshipping Baal and Ashtoreth. Since actions speak louder than words, I want to challenge you," Elijah said! "Bring all the nation of Israel and all of your eight hundred and fifty false prophets to Mount Carmel!"

Soon King Ahab gathered all the children of Israel plus all the false prophets and met on Mount Carmel. Elijah came before all the people and said, "How long will you go back and forth between two beliefs? If the Lord be God, then follow him. But if Baal, then follow him!" Everybody was silent. Then Elijah said, "Bring out two bulls, one for your altar, and one for my altar. We will have a contest. Cut up your bull and lay it on the top of your wood, but with no fire. Next, you will call on your gods. And when it's my turn I will call on the Lord, my God."

The false prophets did as Elijah said. When everything was set up, the false prophets began to call on Baal. They called on him all day, jumping and shouting around the altar! As time passed, Elijah teased them, saying, "Hey, raise your voice louder! Maybe he is busy, or on a trip somewhere! He could be asleep."

So the false prophets continued to cry out to get Baal's attention. They even drew blood by cutting themselves! It was evening time and still no response from Baal! Elijah had enough of all of that noise. So he called the people to where he was. He began to rebuild an altar of God that had been torn down. Elijah used twelve stones to represent the twelve tribes of Israel and stacked them together for the altar. He then put a pile of wood on top. Next, he cut up the bull in pieces, and laid the pieces on top of the wood. Elijah then dug a trench all around the altar and had helpers fill barrels with water. He then told his helpers to pour the water on the bull pieces, and the wood. Everything was soaking wet, and the trench was full of water.

Elijah began to pray. He said, "Lord God of Abraham, Isaac and Israel, let it be known this day, that you are the God of Israel! Also, let it be known that I am your servant, doing your will! Oh Lord, answer me, so that all these people will know that you are the Lord God of Israel!"

Immediately, God showed up with his mighty powers, sending fire down from heaven. The fire was so fierce that it devoured the bull pieces, the wood, the twelve stones, the dust, and every ounce of water in the trench!

After seeing this dramatic display, the people began praising God. They bowed down on their faces and said, "The Lord, He is God! The Lord, He is God!" Right away, the false prophets were taken to the brook Kishon and Elijah killed them all.

Elijah told King Ahab to go up in the mountain and eat and drink because a lot of rain was coming. King Ahab obeyed. Elijah also went back up in the mountains, to Mount Carmel. Here he prayed to God and showed humility to God by dropping to the ground with his face between his knees.

Elijah raised his head and told his servant to go and look out toward the sea. When the servant came back, he told Elijah he did not see anything. So Elijah sent him out again.

In fact, Elijah sent his servant out seven times to look towards the sea. After the seventh time the servant came back and said, "I see a little cloud about the size of a man's hand." Elijah told his servant to go and tell Ahab to get in his chariot and come down from the mountain, or the rain will stop him!

As King Ahab began to ride down from the mountain, the weather turned severe. The sky was black and cloudy. The winds were strong, and the rains were heavy. As all of this was happening, God performed a mighty miracle in Elijah. He gave Elijah extra strength and stamina to run ahead of King Ahab! Keep in mind that Ahab was riding in a chariot pulled by fast moving horses. God allowed Elijah to guide King Ahab safely all the way down from the mountains, to the city of Jezreel.

As soon as King Ahab arrived in the city, he told his wife Jezebel everything that occurred that day. She was very angry about Elijah killing all the prophets who worshipped Baal. Jezebel did not waste any time sending this message to Elijah. She said, "If I don't kill you about this time tomorrow, may the gods kill me!"

When Elijah heard this, he was so afraid. He was always known as a very courageous prophet. He had strong faith and was very obedient to God. After all, God did call him to be a prophet. He was also a rough and tough individual, even in the face of danger. But at this particular time, Elijah was not brave. He hid himself from the evil Queen Jezebel. He ran for his life and traveled many days before entering a cave.

While Elijah stood on the mountain, God allowed three mighty incidents to happen:

1. A strong wind, like a tornado, ripped through the mountains and broke the rocks into pieces.
2. An earthquake happened.
3. A blazing hot fire appeared.

But God did not appear in any of these incidents. Instead, God spoke in a still small voice, saying, "What are you doing here, Elijah?" God listened as Elijah expressed himself. Elijah had experienced much stress. But God's gentle voice and encouraging words were just what he needed. Elijah thought he was the only person in Israel still worshiping God. But God assured him that there were many others who have not bowed down to Baal, but still worshipped God.

Elijah was a true prophet called by God. He was obedient and did exactly what God called him to do throughout his life. As his life on earth was about to end, God commanded Elijah to anoint Elisha as the prophet who would take his place.

God was so pleased with his prophet, Elijah, that He did not allow him to die. God took him straight up to heaven in a whirlwind, in a chariot of fire drawn by horses of fire.

Elisha the prophet saw Elijah taken up in the air. Elijah's mantle fell off of him. Elisha picked the mantle up and that was his last time seeing Elijah.

# Special Feature

**Different Prophets & Prophetesses in the Bible**

**Mariam** – Exodus 15: 20
**Deborah** – Judges Chapters 4 and 5
**Samuel** – 1 Samuel 3
**Elijah** – 1 Kings Chapters 17-19
**Elisha** – 1 Kings 19: 15-21
**Isaiah** – Isaiah Chapter 1
**Jeremiah** – Jeremiah Chapter 1
**Daniel** – Daniel Chapter 2
**Hosea** – Hosea 1:1
**Habakkuk** – Habakkuk 1:1
**Zephaniah** – Zephaniah 1: 1
**Haggai** – Haggai 1:1
**Zechariah** – Zechariah 1: 1
**Malachi** – Malachi 1:1
**Anna** – Luke 2: 36-38
**John the Baptist** – Mark 1: 1-9

# Scripture References

1 Kings 16: 29-33
1 Kings 17: 1-24
1 Kings 18: 1-46
1 Kings 19: 1-3, 9, 11, 13, 15, 16, 18
2 Kings 2:11

# Chapter Review

1. What was going on in Israel when God called Elijah to be his prophet?

2. What kind of woman was Jezebel, and how did she influence her husband, King Ahab?

3. Where did God tell Elijah to go after the brook Cherith dried up?

4. What did the twelve stones represent?

5. Elijah sent his servant out seven times to look towards the sea. True or False?

6. How was Elijah able to guide King Ahab safely down from the mountains?

7. Research and learn more about tornadoes. How do they compare to the strong wind that broke rocks into pieces that God allowed Elijah to see?

# 7

# <u>Jesus</u>

| | |
|---|---|
| **Agitated:** | Visibly upset. |
| **Census:** | A count of all the people and households in an area. |
| **Conceive:** | To become pregnant. |
| **Curious:** | Very eager to know or learn something. |
| **Cycle:** | Something that is repeated often. |
| **Decree:** | A rule that must be carried out, usually issued by a President or King. |
| **Divine:** | Something or someone who is considered Godly. |
| **Emperor:** | A man who rules a kingdom. |
| **Engaged:** | Two people who have promise to marry each other in the future. |
| **Favored:** | A person who is liked a lot. |
| **Fiancé:** | Someone who is engaged to be married. |
| **Foretold:** | Something that is told before it happens. |

**Frankincense:** A very expensive spice, sometimes used as a fragrance in soaps and perfumes.

**Gentiles:** People who are not Jewish.

**God:** A supreme being; the creator of heaven and earth.

**Gospel:** Good news.

**Grace:** Something given to people who don't deserve it.

**Holy:** Something special or sacred for God.

**Holy Spirit:** The third person of the Trinity (God the Father, God the Son, and God the Holy Spirit).

**Humans:** People.

**Inn:** A place to rest or sleep overnight.

**Jews:** A race of people.

**Manger:** A long open box for horses and cattle to eat from.

**Messiah:** A name for the Son of God.

**Miraculous:** A good event that is hard to explain.

**Myrrh:** An oil used for anointing people.

**Original:** The first or beginning of something.

**Overshadow:** To cover someone or something.

**Poverty:** Very poor; a person not having enough basic necessities for living.

**Pregnant:** A woman who has a baby in her belly.

| | |
|---|---|
| **Priests:** | Men in the Bible who conduct or handle special ceremonies. |
| **Proclaimed:** | To make an announcement. |
| **Prosper:** | To grow in health and wealth. |
| **Rabbis:** | A religious teacher in the Jewish race. |
| **Reconcile:** | To make one's relationship with another right again. |
| **Roman Empire:** | A kingdom or country ruled by one person (e.g. an emperor/empress or king/queen). |
| **Scribes:** | People who write. |
| **Shame:** | To be humiliated or embarrassed about something. |
| **Sin:** | Evil actions; breaking God's law (Ten Commandments). |
| **Son of God:** | The person we call Jesus. |
| **Suggested:** | To advise or recommend something to someone. |
| **Summoned:** | To call or send a message for someone to come where you are. |
| **Swaddling clothes:** | Strips of cloth. |
| **Tax:** | Money paid to your government. |
| **Virgin:** | A person who has never had sexual intercourse |

**7**

Jesus
The Son of God

Ever since the Israelites were a nation, they have gone back and forth between obeying and disobeying God. In their obedience, God allowed them to do good and prosper. But in their disobedience, God allowed them to suffer with problems, pain, and defeat. The people would pray and ask God for forgiveness. And God, being the loving God He is, would send them grace and allow them to prosper again. This cycle was repeated over and over again. And as time passed, the Israelites were even more caught up in sin. They were moving further away from God. God sent prophets to tell them to repent and turn from their wicked ways. Many of God's prophets foretold the coming of the Messiah. This Messiah (God's Son) would reconcile the Jewish people back to God. But He would also introduce the Gentiles to God. So when Jesus, The Son of God, did come to earth, His birth was both amazing and very well celebrated.

Jesus had the most amazing birth this world has ever known and will ever know. At the appointed time, God sent his angel, Gabriel, to a small town called Nazareth of Galilee. Here, Gabriel appeared to a young woman named Mary, who was a virgin. Mary was engaged to a man named Joseph. The angel Gabriel said, "Hello favored lady, God is with you." Mary wondered why the angel gave her that type of greeting. Then the angel said, "Do not be afraid, for God is going to bless you in a miraculous way. You will conceive and give birth to a son. And you are to name him Jesus." "How will this happen since I am a virgin," Mary asked. The angel answered her and said, "The Holy Spirit will come upon you and the power of God will overshadow you. This baby that will be born from you is Holy and is The Son of God." The angel also told Mary that her cousin Elizabeth had conceived and would give birth to a son, in her old age. "I am God's servant," said Mary. "May all of what you said come true." Then the angel disappeared.

Mary was very curious about her cousin after the angel told her that Elizabeth was pregnant. So Mary quickly traveled to the hill country of Judea to visit her. Elizabeth was an older woman married to a priest named Zacharias. When Mary walked into the home of Zacharias and Elizabeth, she spoke to them. Then something amazing happened! Elizabeth's baby jumped for joy inside of her and she became filled with the Holy Spirit! Elizabeth exclaimed, "You are blessed among women, and now the mother of my Lord has come to visit me!" And Mary began to praise God.

Mary stayed with Zacharias and Elizabeth for about three months until after their baby was born. Then she went back to Nazareth to see Joseph, her fiancé. Joseph soon found out that Mary was pregnant, and since he was not the father, he was preparing to end their relationship, but in a way that would not shame her. As Joseph thought about this, he fell asleep and an angel of the Lord appeared to him. The angel said, "Don't be afraid to take Mary as your wife, for the child in her is of the Holy Spirit! And she will have a son! You are to name him Jesus, for he will save his people from their sins!" These were some of the same things the angel said to Mary.

Sometime later, a decree went out from Caesar Augustus, who was the Emperor of the Roman Empire. Rome was in control of the world at that time. The decree stated, "All the people of Roman rule must go to their original hometown to be counted in a census, and pay a tax."

Since Joseph and Mary were from the City of David, they both traveled to the town of Bethlehem. By this time, Mary was very close to giving birth. They finally arrived in Bethlehem. But there were so many people there that they could not find a place to stay. I could imagine Joseph saying to the Innkeeper, "But we need a place to stay; she is about to have the baby!" Someone probably suggested the stable, which was at the back of the Inn. With no other choice, they headed to the back of the Inn towards the stable. The Bible doesn't say specifically what animals were there. But I'm thinking probably a cow or two, some birds, a donkey, sheep, and maybe a few goats. These were the types of animals usually found among the people.

That night in the stable, Mary gave birth to a beautiful baby boy. She wrapped her baby in swaddling clothes that she may have prepared before she left home. Then she laid him in a manger.

As Mary and Joseph rested in the stable with their beautiful baby, visitors came in, such as shepherds who had been watching their sheep in the field. The shepherds found out about the baby in a very spectacular way. That night they were in the field watching over their flock when an angel of the Lord came to them! The light around the angel was so bright, that the shepherds were very afraid! But the angel said, "Don't be afraid, I have something good to tell you. For unto you is born this day in the City of David, a Savior, which is Christ the Lord!" Then the angel went on to say, "This is how you will recognize the baby. You will find him wrapped in swaddling clothes and laying in a manger." As the angel was still with the shepherds, all of a sudden, many more angels appeared before the shepherds!

They were singing:

"Glory to God in the highest, and on earth peace, good will toward men!"

After their announcement, the angels went back up to heaven. And the shepherds hurried off to Bethlehem to see the baby. When they got to the stable, they saw Mary and Joseph. They also saw the baby lying in a manger, just as the angel said. They celebrated the baby's birth by going out and telling everyone what they saw and what the angel said about the baby. All the people were amazed at what the shepherds were saying. The shepherds returned to their flocks and praised God for all the things they had seen and heard.

There were several more people who celebrated Jesus' birth. Two of them were in the temple a few weeks later. On that particular day, Mary and Joseph were there to dedicate baby Jesus to God. Simeon was one of those who was expecting the Messiah to come soon. The Holy Spirit told him he would see the Messiah before he died. When Simeon held the baby, he began to praise God. For God let him know that this was the Savior of the world.

The second person in the temple that day was a lady named Anna, who was a prophetess. She began thanking God along with Simeon. She also shared that the Messiah was finally here for those who were expecting the Savior for Jerusalem.

About two years later, wise men who were not Jewish came from the east to visit baby Jesus. They were led to Jerusalem by a star in the sky. When they arrived in Jerusalem, they did not find Jesus. So they asked, "Where is He, that is born King of the Jews? We came to worship him." King Herod, who is the King of Judea, was agitated at hearing that someone else might take his place as King. So he met with the chief priests and scribes to voice his concern. However, they were agitated by the news that Christ would be born in Bethlehem of Judea.

The wise men continued to search for Jesus. But before they could find him, they were summoned to a private meeting with King Herod. After talking to the wise men, the King learned when the star first appeared. The King told them that the baby would be born in Bethlehem. He said, "Go look for the child, and when you have found him, let me know, so that I may come and worship him as well."

So the wise men continued on their journey. Again, the same star which had led them from the east, went before them. The star guided them to the house where the young child was with his parents. As soon as the wise men set foot in the house, they began worshipping the child with gifts. They brought him gold, frankincense and myrrh.

The wise men soon left Jesus. But they did not report back to King Herod. They took another route home. For God told them in a dream to do so.

Sometime after the wise men left, an angel appeared to Joseph in a dream. He said, "Get up! Take the young child and His mother and run off to Egypt! For King Herod will try to kill the child!" Sure enough, Herod saw that he was tricked by the wise men. He was very angry and had many young boys, two years old and under, killed. This was because he really wanted to make sure Baby Jesus was dead.

King Herod did not succeed at killing the Son of God. In fact, he eventually died while Jesus and his parents were still in Egypt. In another dream, an angel told Joseph it was safe for him and his family to return to Israel. While in Israel, Joseph learned that Herod's son Archelaus was now King of Judea. So Joseph was afraid to go there. Instead, God allowed them to go and live in Nazareth of Galilee.

For years the Jewish nation had heard of the coming of the Messiah. This Messiah would come from the tribe of Judah. He would be born from the line of David, a King that will rule forever.

But so many of God's people had turned away from him. God loves all of us so much. His desire is that all would be saved. He did not choose the children of Israel because they were special; no! He chose them so that they would set the example and lead the way for others to have a closer relationship with Him. The leaders of the Jewish people were allowing their selfishness to lead them down the wrong road. These were mostly priests and rabbis. They should have been the first to embrace the coming of the Messiah and share the Gospel of Christ. But they did not want anyone else to know as much as they knew. Not only did God let the

Jewish people know that He was sending His Son to earth, but he let the Gentiles know as well.

Even though Jesus was the Son of God, God allowed him to be born in poverty. When I think of God, I imagine someone who is rich and famous. But Jesus' parents were poor. Outside of love, they did not have much to offer him. But it does not matter how Jesus was born, or where He was born. The fact is, He was born for a very special purpose. He was God's very own Son. "For God so loved the world, that he gave his only begotten Son, that whosoever believe in him should not perish, but have everlasting life (John 3:16)." Baby Jesus was not just human, but He was also Devine. In other words, He was to represent God in the flesh. The Jewish people and others knew that Baby Jesus would grow up and influence the whole world in a significant way. Jesus would also live a servant's life before the people. He would die for the sins of the world. But then, He would soon return and be our King for all eternity.

# Special Feature

### Christmas
*By Kay E. McNeil*

Christmas is a symbol of love,
    because of what took place.
The God of Heaven gave his Son
    to save the human race.

It was a very humble birth,
    the baby Jesus had.
Lying in a manger of a stable,
    that precious little lad.

It seemed as if He didn't have much,
    but really, he had it all.
To be born the King of the universe,
    and save mankind from its fall.

In giving His Son to us God showed,
    the deepest of all love.
For to give up an only child,
    could only come from above.

During Christmas time remember this,
    it's not the material things.
Christmas is a symbol of love,
    because Jesus was born our King.

# Bible Verses Used

Matthew 1: 18-25
Matthew 2: 1-23
Luke 1: 26-45
LUKE 2: 1-38
John 3: 16

# Chapter Review

1. What cycle did the Israelites repeat over and over again?

2. When did Elizabeth's baby jump for joy?

3. Where did Joseph and Mary have to go to be counted in the census?

4. How did the shepherds celebrate the birth of Jesus?

5. Did the three wise men obey King Herod? Yes or No?

6. Why did King Herod have many young boys killed who were two years old and under?

7. Do you think adults can become successful in life, even though they were born and grew up poor? How?

www.ingramcontent.com/pod-product-compliance
Lightning Source LLC
Chambersburg PA
CBHW072204090426
42740CB00012B/2377